BAYONET TRAINING

1918

(1916 Reprinted with Amendments)

Issued by the General Staff.

The Naval & Military Press Ltd

Published by the
The Naval & Military Press
in association with the Royal Armouries

Unit 10 Ridgewood Industrial Park,
Uckfield, East Sussex, TN22 5QE
Tel: +44 (0) 1825 749494
Fax: +44 (0) 1825 765701

MILITARY HISTORY AT YOUR FINGERTIPS
www.naval-military-press.com

ONLINE GENEALOGY RESEARCH
www.military-genealogy.com

ONLINE MILITARY CARTOGRAPHY
www.militarymaproom.com

ROYAL
ARMOURIES

The Library & Archives Department at the Royal Armouries Museum, Leeds, specialises in the history and development of armour and weapons from earliest times to the present day. Material relating to the development of artillery and modern fortifications is held at the Royal Armouries Museum, Fort Nelson.

For further information contact:
Royal Armouries Museum, Library, Armouries Drive,
Leeds, West Yorkshire LS10 1LT
Royal Armouries, Library, Fort Nelson, Down End Road, Fareham PO17 6AN

Or visit the Museum's website at
www.armouries.org.uk

In reprinting in facsimile from the original, any imperfections are inevitably reproduced and the quality may fall short of modern type and cartographic standards.

$\dfrac{40}{\text{W.O.}}$
6501

BAYONET TRAINING.

1918.

(1916 Reprinted with Amendments.)

Issued by the General Staff.

Printed under the authority of His Majesty's Stationery Office
By HARRISON AND SONS,
PRINTERS IN ORDINARY TO HIS MAJESTY,
ST. MARTIN'S LANE, LONDON, W.C. 2.

TABLE OF CONTENTS.

B 13793)　Wt. w. 430—P.P. 994　100м　4/18　H & S　P. 18/304

BAYONET TRAINING, 1918.

SECTION 1.

SPECIAL FEATURES OF THE BAYONET.

1. To attack with the bayonet effectively requires **Good Direction, Strength and Quickness**, during a state of wild excitement and probably physical exhaustion. The limit of the range of a bayonet is about 5 feet (measured from the opponent's eyes), but more often the killing is at close quarters, at a range of 2 feet or less, when troops are struggling *corps à corps* in trenches or darkness. *Essential points of the bayonet.*

The bayonet is essentially an offensive weapon—go straight at an opponent with the point threatening his throat and deliver the point wherever an opening presents itself. If no opening is obvious, one must be created by beating off the opponent's weapon or making a "feint point" in order to make him uncover himself.

2. Hand-to-hand fighting with the bayonet is individual, which means that a man must think and act for himself and rely on his own resource and skill; but, as in games, he must play for his side and not only for himself. In a bayonet assault all ranks go forward to kill, and only those who have developed skill and strength by constant training will be able to kill. *Hand-to-hand fighting.*

3. The spirit of the bayonet must be inculcated into all *The spirit of the bayonet.*

(B 13793)   A

ranks so that they go forward with that aggressive determination and confidence of superiority born of continual practice, without which a bayonet assault will not be effective.

Continuity of training.

4. The technical points of bayonet fighting are extremely few and simple The essence of bayonet training is continuity of practice.

SECTION 2.

METHOD OF CARRYING OUT BAYONET TRAINING AND HINTS TO INSTRUCTORS.

Development of the individual.

5. An important point to be kept in mind in bayonet training is the development of the individual by teaching him to think and act for himself. The simplest means of attaining this end is to make men use their brains and eyes to the fullest extent by carrying out the practices, so far as possible, without words of command, i.e., to point at a shifting target as soon as it is stationary, to parry sticks, &c. The class should, whenever possible, work in pairs and act on the principle of "Master and Pupil." This procedure, in itself, develops individuality and confidence. Sharp jerky words of command, which tend to make men act mechanically, should be omitted. Rapidity of movement and alertness are taught by competition in fixing and unfixing the bayonet and by other such "quickening movements."

Duration of lessons and practices.

6. As the technique of bayonet fighting is so simple, long detail is quite unnecessary and makes the work monotonous. All instruction should be carried out on common sense lines. It should seldom be necessary to give the detail of a "point" or "parry" more than two or three times, after which the classes should acquire the correct positions by practice. For

this reason a lesson or daily practice should rarely last more than half-an-hour. Remember that nothing kills interest so easily as monotony.

7. The spirit of the bayonet is to be inculcated by describing the special features of bayonet and hand-to-hand fighting. The men must learn to practise bayonet fighting in the spirit and with the enthusiasm which animate them when training for their games, and to look upon their instructor as a trainer and helper. *Spirit of the bayonet.*

8. Interest in the work is to be created by explaining the reasons for the various positions, the method of handling the rifle and bayonet, and the uses of the "points." Questions should be put to the men to find out whether they understand these reasons. When men realise the object of their work they naturally take a greater interest in it. *Work made interesting.*

9. Progression in bayonet training is regulated by obtaining first correct positions and good direction, then quickness. Strength is the outcome of continual practice. *Progression.*

10. In order to encourage dash and gradually strengthen the leg muscles from the commencement of the training, classes should be frequently practised in charging short distances. *Cultivate dash and vigour.*

11. All company officers and N.C.Os. should be taught how to instruct in bayonet training in order that they may be able to teach their platoons and sections this very important part of a soldier's training, which must be regularly practised during the whole of his service at home, and during his periods of rest behind the firing line. *Officers' and N.C.Os.' classes.*

12. Sacks for dummies should be filled with vertical layers of straw and thin sods (grass or heather), leaves, shavings, &c., in such a way as to give the greatest resistance without injury to the bayonet. A realistic effect, necessitating a strong withdrawal as if gripped by a bone, is obtained by *Sacks*

(B 13793)   A 2

4

inseiting a vertical layer of pieces of hard wood, ¼-inch thick (old cheese cases, oak palings, &c.), between the stuffing and the sack on the side facing the attacker; only one layer of wood is to be used, and the grain must be vertical.

These sack dummies can be made to stand on end by fixing a wooden cross or star (two or three pieces of wood about 2 inches broad and ¾ inch thick nailed across one another) in the base of the sack before filling it. They can also be placed with good effect on rough tripods, or tied to improvised stools. Dummy sacks should be hung from gallows by a double suspension from the cross-bar to the top corners and weighted or tethered to the ground from the bottom corners.

Care of weapons.

13. The greatest care should be taken that the object representing the opponent and its support should be incapable of injuring the bayonet or butt. Only light sticks are to be used for parrying practice.

The chief causes of injury to the bayonet are insufficient instruction in the bayonet training lessons, failure to withdraw the bayonet clear of the dummy before advancing, and placing the dummies on hard unprepared ground.

Care of apparatus.

14. The upkeep and proper filling of dummies, and the repair of assault practice courses, form part of the duties of Army Gymnastic Staff and Assistant Instructors.

Discs.

15. For practising direction there must always be an aiming mark on the dummy. Cardboard discs for this purpose are supplied by the Stationery Office. By continually changing the position of the mark the " life " of the dummies is considerably prolonged. Should the supply of discs fail, they can be improvised out of cardboard or thick paper, or five or six numbers can be painted on the dummies as marks.

SECTION 3.

PRELIMINARY BAYONET LESSONS.

16. Open ranks for bayonet practice as follows :—"Rear Class Rank—About turn"; "Odd numbers of the front rank and arrange-even numbers of the rear rank—Six (or more) paces forward —March," "About turn"; "The whole, one pace right close—March." Or, "For Bayonet practice open—out."

Small classes should be opened out from single rank.

Classes should always work with bayonets fixed.

When teaching a new position, face the class to a flank and let them "rest." First show them the position, explaining essential points and giving the reasons for them. Then show the position a second time, making the class observe each movement, so that, from the very commencement of the bayonet training, a man is taught to use his eyes and brain. Face the ranks and order them to assume the position explained and shown. *Pick out the man who shows the best position and let the class look at and copy him.* Remember that his position may not be ideal, but it is more correct than those assumed by the remainder, who, being beginners, cannot distinguish the difference between a good position and an ideal one. Many instructors err by trying to get a class of beginners to idealise at once.

17. The Recruit's Course consists of five lessons and the Recruit's Final Assault Practice. The hours in the syllabus for Course. bayonet training are so divided as to give daily practice. The training should be carried out chiefly in a "free and easy" kit, but men should be accustomed to use their bayonets when wearing belt and pouches ; packs and box respirators may be worn when an efficiency test is in progress.

For the "pointing" and "parrying" practices a light stick, 5 feet to 5 feet 9 inches long and 2½ inches to 4 inches in circumference, with thrusting ring and pad, must be provided for every two men.

Daily Practice. 18. Half-an-hour a day, on at least five days a week, should be devoted to the daily practice in bayonet fighting by trained soldiers. By this daily practice · accuracy of direction, quickness, and strength are developed, and a soldier is accustomed to using the bayonet under conditions which approximate to actual fighting. This half-hour should be apportioned to (1) Pointing at the body ; (2) Pointing at thrusting rings, &c., on light sticks at varying distances and directions ; (3) Parrying light sticks ; (4) Dummy work ; (5) Counter charges ; and (6) when sufficiently proficient, the Final Assault Practice.

LESSON 1.

"On Guard." 19. Point of the bayonet directed at the base of the opponent's throat, the rifle held easily and naturally with both hands, the barrel inclined slightly (about 30°) to the left, the right hand, over the navel, grasping the small of the butt, the left hand holding the rifle at the most convenient position in front of the backsight so that the left arm is only slightly bent, *i e.*, the upper arm and fore-arm making an angle of about 150°. The legs well separated in a natural position, such as a man walking might adopt on meeting with resistance, *i.e.*, left knee slightly bent, right toe inclined to the right front.

The position should not be constrained in any way but be one of aggression, alertness, and readiness to go forward for immediate attack (*vide* Plate I).

The "On guard" position will also be taught with the right foot in front.

Common Faults.

(1) **Leaning** body back.
(2) **Left arm** too much bent.
(3) **Right hand** held too low and too **far back**.
(4) **Rifle** grasped **too** rigidly, restraining all freedom **of** movement.

Assume a position of "rest" in the easiest way without "Rest." moving the feet.

The hands holding the rifle as when on guard; the left "High wrist level with, and directly in front of, the left shoulder; port." right hand level with and to the right of the buckle of the waist-belt.

When jumping ditches, surmounting obstacles, &c., the position of the rifle should be approximately maintained with the left hand alone, leaving the right hand free.

20. Grasping the rifle firmly, vigorously deliver the point "Long from the "on guard" position to the full extent of the left Point." arm, butt running alongside and kept close to the right forearm. Body inclined forward; left knee well bent; right leg braced, and weight of the body pressed well forward with the fore part of the right foot, heel raised.

The chief power in a "point" is derived from the right arm with the weight of the body behind it, the left arm being used more to direct the point of the bayonet. The eyes must be fixed on the object at which the point is directed. In making "points" other than straight to the front, the left foot should move laterally in the same direction as that in which the "point" is made.

During the later stages of this lesson the men should be practised in stepping forward with the rear foot when delivering the "point."

Common Faults.

(1) Rifle drawn back before delivering the " point."
(2) Butt of the rifle held as high as or against the right shoulder.
(3) The eyes not directed on the object.
(4) Left knee not sufficiently bent.
(5) Body not thrust sufficiently forward.
(6) Right heel kept on ground.

Remarks.

The " with-drawal."

The " long point " is made against an opponent at a range of about four to five feet from the attacker's eye.

21. To withdraw the bayonet after a " long point " has been delivered, draw the rifle straight back until the right hand is well behind the hip, and immediately resume the " on guard " position. If the leverage or proximity to the object transfixed renders it necessary, the left hand must first be slipped up close to the piling-swivel, and, when a pupil reaches the stage of delivering a " point " while advancing on a dummy, he will adopt this method.

After every " point," a rapid " withdrawal," essential to quick work with the bayonet, should be practised before returning to the " on guard " position.

Progression.

1st practice. Pointing at parts of the body.

22. Men should always be made to point at a target, e.g., at a named part of the body of the opposite man : " At the right eye " (long pause to commence with), " point " (a pause), " withdraw." Oblique " points " should be practised by pointing at the men to the right and left fronts.

As progress is made, the pause between the " point " and the " withdrawal " should be shortened until the men reach a stage when they "withdraw " and come "on guard" directly after making a " point," judging their own time. They should be taught to point at two or more parts of the body, e.g., "First at the nose, then at the right thigh—point."

To practise action against a retreating foe, turn the inside ranks about and let them "rest." Show the position of the kidneys (small of the back, either side of the spine), and make the outside ranks point at those of the inside ranks, and vice versâ.

23. If possible, the point 'of the bayonet should be directed against an opponent's throat, especially in corps à corps fighting, as the point will enter easily and make a fatal wound on penetrating a few inches and, being near the eyes, makes an opponent "funk." Other vulnerable and usually exposed parts are the face, chest, lower abdomen and thighs, and the region of the kidneys when the back is turned. Four to six inches' penetration is sufficient to incapacitate and allow for a quick withdrawal, whereas if a bayonet is driven home too far it is often impossible to withdraw it. In such cases a round should be fired to break up the obstruction. *Vulnerable parts of the body.*

24. The class, working in pairs, with the Instructor supervising, should be practised in pointing in various directions, e.g., (1) at the opposite man's hand, which he places in various positions on and off his body ; (2) at thrusting rings, &c., tied on the ends of sticks. *2nd practice. Pointing at changing targets.*

This practice should be done without word of command, so that the eye and brain may be trained.

25. The men will be taught to transfix a disc or number painted on a dummy, first at a distance of about five feet from the dummy (i.e., the extreme range of the bayonet), and then after advancing three or more paces. The advance *3rd practice. Pointing at discs on dummies.*

must be made in a practical and natural way, and should be practised with either foot to the front when the "point" is delivered.

The rifle must never be drawn back when making a "long point" in a forward movement. The impetus of the body and the forward stretching of the arms supply sufficient force.

The bayonet must be withdrawn immediately after the "point" has been delivered, and a forward threatening attitude be assumed to the side of or beyond the dummy.

Unless the rifle is firmly gripped it is liable to injure the hand.

To guard against accidents the men must be at least five feet apart when the practice is carried out collectively.

The principles of this practice will be observed when pointing at dummies in trenches, standing upright on the ground, or suspended on gallows. They should be applied at first slowly and deliberately, for no attempt must be made to carry out the Final Assault Practice before the men have been carefully instructed in, and have thoroughly mastered, the preliminary lessons.

Lesson 2.

The Right and Left Parry.

"Right (left) parry.

26. From the position of "On guard," vigorously straighten the left arm without bending the wrist or twisting the rifle in the hand, and force the rifle forward far enough to the right (left) to fend off the adversary's weapon.

The eyes must be kept on the weapon which is being parried.

Common Faults.

(1) Wide sweeping parry with no forward movement in it.

(2) Eyes taken off the weapon to be parried.

Men should be taught to regard the parry as part of an offensive movement, namely, of the " point " or butt stroke which would immediately follow it in actual combat. For this reason, as soon as the movements of the parries have been learnt they should always be accompanied with a slight forward movement of the body.

Parries will be practised with the right as well as with the left foot forward, preparatory to the practice of parrying when advancing.

27. Men when learning the parries should be made to observe the movements of the rifle carefully, and should not be kept longer at this practice than is necessary for them to understand what is required, that is vigorous, yet controlled, action. *1st practice. Parries by word of command.*

The class works in pairs with scabbards on bayonets, one man pointing with the stick and the other parrying ; the " on-guard " position is resumed after each parry. At first this practice must be slow and deliberate, without being allowed to become mechanical, and will be progressively increased in rapidity and vigour. *2nd practice. Parrying light sticks.*

Later, a " point " at that part of the body indicated by the opposite man's hand should immediately follow the right parry ; and, since the point cannot be kept on the opponent after a left parry, this should be followed by a butt stroke.

The men must also be taught to parry points made at them :—(1) by an " enemy " in a trench when they are themselves on the parapet ; (2) by an " enemy " on the parapet when they are in the trench, and ; (3) when both are fighting on the same level at close quarters in a deep trench.

3rd practice.
Parry stick and point at dummy.

Finally, sticks long enough to represent the opponent's weapon in the "on guard" position should be attached to the dummies and parried before delivering the "point."

Lesson 3.
The Short Point.

"Short point."

28. Shift the left hand quickly towards the muzzle and draw the rifle back to the full extent of the right arm, the butt either upwards or downwards according as a low or a high point is to be made; then deliver the "point" vigorously to the full extent of the left arm.

N.B.—The "short point" is used at a range of about three feet, and in close fighting it is the natural "point" to make when the bayonet has just been withdrawn after a "long point." If a strong "withdrawal" is necessary the right hand should be slipped above the backsight after the "short point" has been made.

Practice.

29. The principles of the three practices of Lesson 1 should be observed so far as they apply. By placing two discs on a dummy the "short point" should be taught in conjunction with the "long point," the first disc being transfixed with the latter, the second with the former point. On delivery of the "long point" if the left foot is forward, the "short point" would take place with the right foot forward, and *vice versâ*.

Parries will be practised from the position of the "short point."

Lesson 4.
Jab or Upward Point.

The "jab" or "upward point."

30. From the position of the "short point" shift the right hand up the rifle and grasp it above or below the backsight, according to range of target, at the same time bringing the rifle to an almost vertical position close to the body, and, from this position, bend the knees and jab the point of the bayonet upwards into the throat or under the chin of the opponent. The bent arms should be kept rigid and the movement made from the shoulders.

Common Faults.

(1) Rifle drawn backward and not held upright enough.

(2) "Point" made with sweeping upward action and relaxed muscles.

From the "jab" position men will be practised in fending off an attack made on any part of them by an opponent.

When making a "jab" from the "on guard" position, the right, being the thrusting hand, will be brought up first.

The jab can be employed successfully in close-quarter fighting in narrow trenches and when "embraced" by an opponent.

LESSON 5.

METHODS OF INJURING AN OPPONENT.

31. It should be impressed upon the class that, although a man's "point" has missed or has been parried, or his bayonet has been broken, he can, as "attacker," still maintain his advantage by injuring his opponent in one of the ways described in paras. 32–35.

32. UPWARD OR UPPERCUT BUTT STROKE.—Swing the butt up at the opponent's fork, ribs, forearm, &c., using a half arm blow and advancing the rear foot. *Butt strokes.*

FORWARD BUTT STROKE.—If the opponent jumps back so that the first butt stroke misses, the rifle will come into horizontal position over the left shoulder, butt leading; the attacker will then step in with the rear foot and dash the butt into his opponent's face.

SLASH STROKE.—If the opponent retires still further out

of distance, the attacker again closes up and slashes his bayonet down on his opponent's head or neck.

OVERHAND BUTT STROKE.—If the point is beaten or brought down, the butt can be used effectively by crashing it down on the opponent's head with an over-arm blow, advancing the rear foot. When the opponent is out of distance, the Slash Stroke can again be used.

In individual fighting the butt can also be used horizontally against the opponent's ribs, forearm, &c. This method is impossible in trench fighting or in an attack, owing to the horizontal sweep of the bayonet to the attacker's left.

It should be clearly understood that the butt must not be employed when it is possible to use the point of the bayonet effectively.

Butt Strokes should be practised in "second intention," *i.e.*, as a second attack after the first attack with point has been parried.

33. The Upward or Uppercut Butt Stroke is essentially a half-arm blow from the shoulder, keeping the elbow rigid, and it can, therefore, be successfully employed only when the right hand is grasping the rifle at the small of the butt.

34. Butt strokes can only be used in certain circumstances and positions, but if men acquire absolute control of their weapons under these conditions they will be able to adapt themselves to all other phases of in-fighting. For instance, when a man is gripped by an opponent so that neither the point nor the butt can be used, the knee brought up against the fork or the heel stamped on the instep may momentarily disable him and make him release his hold.

Tripping.　**35.** When wrestling, the opponent can be tripped by forcing his weight on to one leg and kicking that leg away from under him, or any other wrestler's trip, *e.g.*, "back-heel," may be used.

N.B.—The above methods will only temporarily disable an enemy, who must be killed with the bayonet.

PRACTICE.

36. When the classes have been shown the methods of using the butt and the knee they should be practised on the padded stick. Fix several discs on a dummy and make a point at one, use the knee on another fixed low down, jab a third, and so on.

Light dummies should be used for practice with the butt, in order to avoid damage to it.

SECTION 4.

TACTICAL APPLICATION OF THE BAYONET.

37. A bayonet assault should preferably be made under cover of fire, surprise, or darkness. In these circumstances the prospect of success is greatest, for a bayonet is useless at any range except hand-to-hand. *Practical use of the bayonet.*

38. At night all these forms of cover can be utilised. On the other hand, confusion is inherent in fighting by night; consequently, the execution of a successful night attack with the bayonet requires considerable and lengthy training. Units should be frequently practised in night work with the bayonet. *Night work.*

39. The bayonet is essentially a weapon of offence which must be used with skill and vigour; otherwise it has but little effect. To await passively an opportunity of using the bayonet entails defeat, since an approaching enemy will merely stand out of bayonet range and shoot down the defenders. *Bayonet an offensive weapon.*

40. In an assault the enemy should be killed with the bayonet. Firing should be avoided, for in the mix-up a bullet, after passing through an opponent's body, may kill a friend who happens to be in the line of fire. *No firing during an assault.*

FINAL ASSAULT PRACTICE.

41. This practice is only to be carried out after the men have been thoroughly trained in all the preliminary lessons, and have acquired complete control of their weapons, otherwise injury to rifles and bayonets will result from improper application of the methods laid down in the foregoing instruction.

The Final Assault Practice must approximate as nearly as possible to the conditions of actual fighting.

Nervous tension due to the anticipation of an attack, reacting on the body, as well as the advance across the open and the final dash at the enemy, combine to tire an assaulting party. It is only by their physical fitness and superior skill in the use of the bayonet that they can overcome a comparatively fresh foe.

Therefore quick aim and good direction of the bayonet, when moving rapidly or even when surmounting obstacles, accurate delivery of a point of sufficient strength and vigour to penetrate clothing and equipment, clean withdrawal of the bayonet—which requires no small effort, especially should it be fixed by a bone—are of the greatest importance, and need the same careful attention and constant practice as are devoted to obtaining efficiency with the rifle.

In the Final Assault Practice the charge brings the men to the first trench in a comparatively exhausted condition, and the accuracy of the aim is tested by the disc, which can only be "carried" by a true and vigorous thrust and a clean withdrawal.

For this practice the men should be made to begin the assault from a trench six or seven feet deep, as well as from the open, and they should not cheer until close up to the "enemy."

17

42. A reproduction of a labyrinth of trenches, with dummies in the "dug-outs" and shelters between the trenches, forms an excellent Final Assault Practice Course. Assaults should be made from all four sides in order to give variety. The edges of the trenches should be protected by spars or baulks anchored back; otherwise constant use will soon wear them out. Cinders scattered over the course prevent the men from slipping. If gallows cannot be erected, sack dummies should be placed on tripods or on end, as well as lying in trenches or on the parapets, with soft earth free from stones under them. *(Final Assault Practice Course.)*

For preliminary practice it is advisable to use a well-defined enemy trench as the objective, with firm ground over which the attacking squads may advance.

During the later stages of training, however, men should be practised to assault overground, which more nearly represents the conditions which obtain after a heavy bombardment of the enemy's trenches.

Commanding Officers will be responsible for the construction of the Final Assault Practice Courses, and will decide on the number, length, and nature of the trenches in accordance with the ground available. Officers in charge of Physical and Bayonet Training, or where there are no such officers Army Gymnastic Staff and Assistant Instructors, will be responsible to Commanding Officers for the upkeep of the courses.

43. Practical schemes should be arranged by combining the Final Assault Practice with other branches of training on lines laid down in S.S. 185, "Assault Training," Sept., 1917. *(Tactical schemes.)*

44. Competitions can be arranged by allotting or deducting marks for (1) number of discs transfixed and carried on a bayonet, (2) time taken from giving the signal to charge until the last man of the team passes the finishing post, and (3) style. *(Competitions.)*

Competitions should never be carried out until the men have completed their lessons in bayonet training and thoroughly mastered the handling of the bayonet in the Final Assault Practice.

SECTION 5.

TACTICAL PRINCIPLES TO BE OBSERVED DURING BAYONET TRAINING.

METHOD OF CARRYING RIFLE WITH BAYONET FIXED.

45. *Quick Short Advance* (in the open).

The rifle will be held at the "High Port."

This position is suitable for close formation, minimises risk of accidents when surmounting obstacles, and can be maintained with the left hand alone, allowing free use of the right when necessary. It is also the best method of keeping the rifle clean when crossing marshy ground or deep mud.

46. *Long Advance* (close formation).

The rifle will be slung over the left shoulder, sling to the front and perpendicular to the ground.

This is a safe method of carrying the rifle and allowing the free use of both hands.

47. *Long Advance* (open order).

The rifle will be carried at "the trail."

THE ASSAULT.

48. The importance of discipline and organised control throughout the conduct of a bayonet assault cannot be over emphasised. It must be remembered that in this, as in all other military operations, success can only be achieved through the closest co-operation of all concerned; and that, while individual initiative is not to be discouraged, it must be strictly subordinated to the intention of the leader of the assaulting party.

Men should be shown by demonstration that it is in their own interests to pay attention to this point, and that the failure of an enterprise can usually be traced to the lack of this close co-operation.

49. During training the following general principles will be observed :—

i. All members of the attacking party must leave the trench or rise from cover simultaneously.

In addition to the advantages of surprise needless casualties are thereby avoided.

ii. The first stage, especially of a long advance, will be slow and steady—not faster than the pace of the slowest man.

Such an advance has a decided moral effect on the enemy, makes certain of the maximum shock at the moment of impact, and at the same time allows the attacking force to reach its objective without undue exhaustion. On the other hand, if the assault is allowed to develop without control and in a haphazard fashion, the moral effect of a steady resistless wall of men is lost, and the defenders may be given time to dispose of their opponents in detail.

50. The actual charge will not be made over a greater distance than twenty paces. Within the last ten yards and before closing with the enemy the rifle will be brought to the threatening, yet defensive, "on guard." Line will as far as possible be maintained until actual contact with the enemy is gained.

51. As soon as the position has been taken, and prior to any attack on a further position or any other operation whatsoever, the infantry must be reformed as explained in Infantry Training, Section **124**, 4, ammunition being re-distributed and every precaution being taken against a counter-attack. In trench warfare indiscriminate pursuit with the bayonet must never be allowed unless orders to that

effect have been given by the leader of the assaulting party
The attacking troops are not so fresh as the enemy, and
experience has shown that unorganised pursuit lends itself to
ambush and casualties from machine gun fire. In most cases
the work of immediate pursuit is better done by the support-
ing artillery—the infantry assisting by rapid fire on the
retreating enemy.

ASSAULT PRACTICE.

52. A useful form of Final Assault Practice which can be
adapted to a variety of "special ideas" is described in
paras. 53–55.

The following materials are assumed :—

A. Communicating trenches leading to a fire trench with
an open space in front.

B. An occupied enemy trench.

C. Gallows with dummies, representing the enemy,

  (i) retiring from " B," or
  (ii) coming up in support of " B," or
  (iii) making a counter-attack on the captured trench
    " B."

53. (i) The attacking party makes a controlled assault
on " A," which is cleared of the enemy.

(ii) It is then reformed and an assault is launched on
" B," after taking which

(iii) " C " is regarded in one or other of the above ways,
and action taken accordingly.

54. Throughout the training men must be constantly
practised in :—

i. The recognised method of carrying the rifle with
bayonet fixed.

ii. Rapid advance out of deep trenches.

iii. Control and maintenance of line and opening of fire during an advance.

iv. Using the bayonet with effect in the cramped space of communicating and fire trenches.

v. Reforming and opening of fire after the assault.

vi. Acting as leaders of attacking party.

55. Instructors should endeavour by every means in their power to arouse the interest and imagination of their men during the assault practice. The "special idea" to be adopted should invariably be explained beforehand.

Each dummy must be regarded as an actual armed opponent, and each line of dummies as an enemy line attacking, defending or retiring, and be disposed of accordingly.

Any tendency towards carelessness and slackness must be instantly checked, and it should be impressed on all ranks that a practice assault which is not carried out with the necessary quickness, vigour and determination is worse than useless.

Lack of imagination, which allows men and their leaders to violate the most elementary principles of tactics in practice assaults against dummies, can only lead to disaster in a real assault against the enemy.

SECTION 6.

GENERAL INSTRUCTIONS FOR BAYONET TRAINING PRACTICE.

(a) "On guard," "withdraw," all points and parries, and the "jab," will be taught first with the left, then with the right foot forward.

(b) The "starting position" for a "short point" is shown

in Plate IV. All "short points" will be practised from this position, which must be marked, except after a "point" into a dummy, by a momentary pause so as to break men of the habit of drawing back the rifle from "on guard" before making a "point."

(c) From the outset squads will be frequently practised in charging for short distances in the open – as a strengthening exercise for the legs and a quickening exercise.

(d) A target to point at will always be named when working by word of command ; it will be indicated by the position of the hand when working in class; and it will be clearly marked on all dummies.

(e) When working in ranks the distance apart must be sufficient to avoid all danger of accident when the "points" are being made. When "points" have been made advancing, the ranks will change position by coming to the "high port," doubling past each other right shoulder to right shoulder, and turning about. When working against dummies, men will always continue the movement past the dummy, which they will leave on their right.

(f) The "withdrawal," once taught, will be made after each "point." After a "point," advancing rear foot or on the advance, the hand will always be moved up the rifle, but in the 1st and 2nd practices, since the arm and body are already stretched to their full extent, and the left hand cannot move further forward, the hand will be shifted after the "withdrawal" from the "long point."

(g) All sticks must be padded at one end.

(h) In the third practices the "points" will also be practised deliberately and progressively on dummies placed, as a preparation for the Final Assault Course, in positions of increasing difficulty, e.g., on parapets and steps of shallow trenches, and in fire and communicating trenches.

(*i*) Scabbards will not be removed from the **bayonet** **except** for pointing at dummies.

SECTION 7.

SUMMARY OF PROGRESSIVE STEPS.

(1) Class arrangements.
(2) Explain hand-to-hand fighting and inculcate **the** spirit of the bayonet.

LESSON 1.

(3) On guard. (Plate I.)
(4) Rest.
(5) High port.

1st Practice. (In class, by word of command.)

(6) " Long point."
(7) " Withdrawal "; (*a*) after stationary " point"; (*b*) after " point " advancing rear foot (Plate III). (First demonstrated by Instructor on a dummy.)
(8) Oblique " long point."
(9) " Long point," followed by " long point " advancing rear foot.
(10) Vulnerable spots explained ; region of the kidneys shown ; class practised in making " points " at tnese.

2nd Practice. (Class working by eye.)

(11) " Long point."
(12) " Long point," followed by " long point " advancing rear foot.

(13) Varied direct and oblique "long points" at thrusting ring.

3rd Practice. (Pointing at dummy.)

(14) "Long point" (Plate II).
(15) "Long point" advancing rear foot.
(16) Advance, "long point."
(17) Advance, "long points" (at two or more dummies).

LESSON 2.

(18) Explain value of parries : how, in charging, the parry must be strong enough to beat aside opponent's weapon.

1st Practice. (In class, by word of command.)

(19) Explain, and make the class perform, the movements required for the various parries.

2nd Practice. (Class working by eye.)

(20) Parry stick pointed at the breast.
(21) Parry stick pointed at the breast and point.
(22) Parry stick pointed at head, body or legs.
(23) Parry stick pointed in varying order at head, body or legs, and point.
(24) When standing in a trench, parry "point" made with stick from above.
(25) When standing on a parapet, parry "point" made with stick by man in trench.
(26) With stick parry "point" made with stick by advancing opponent.
(27) With stick parry "point" made with stick by advancing opponent, and point.

(28) With stick, parry "point" made with stick lightly held in one hand by charging opponent. (By holding his stick in the right hand the attacker will show he is pointing at the left side of the defender, who will make a left parry, and vice versa. To avoid defender's weapon, the attacker will pass on the side opposite to the parry.)

3rd Practice. (Pointing at dummy with stick representing opponent's weapon.)

(29) Advance, parry stick and point.

Lesson 3.

(30) Demonstrate "short point," and explain when it is used (Plate IV).

1st Practice. (In class, by word of command.)

(31) "Short point."
(32) "Withdrawal"; (*a*) stationary; (*b*) advancing rear foot. (Demonstrated by Instructor on dummy.)
(33) Oblique "short point."
(34) "Short point" advancing rear foot.
(35) "Long point" advancing rear foot, followed by "short point" advancing rear foot.

2nd Practice. (Class working by eye.)

(36) "Short point."
(37) "Short point" advancing rear foot.
(38) "Long point" advancing rear foot, followed by "short point" advancing rear foot.
(39) Varied direct and oblique "long and short points" at thrusting ring.
(40) Practise various parries, parries and "points," from "short point" position.

3rd Practice. (Pointing at dummy.)

(41) " Short point."
(42) " Short point " advancing rear foot.
(43) " Long point " advancing rear foot ; "short point "
advancing rear foot.
(44) Advance, " long point," " short point " (at two
dummies in suitable positions).

LESSON 4.

(45) Demonstrate " jab " at dummy : then, by placing
men of the squad in suitable positions, explain
when and how it is used in conjunction with
" points " (Plate V).

1st Practice. (In class, by word of command.)

(46) " Jab," from " jab " position.
(47) " Short point " advancing rear foot, " jab " advancing
rear foot.
(48) " Long point " advancing rear foot, " jab " advancing
rear foot.
(49) " Long point " advancing rear foot, "short point "
advancing rear foot, " jab " advancing rear foot.
(50) " Short point " advancing rear foot, " jab " advancing
rear foot, " long point " advancing rear foot.

2nd Practice. (Class working by eye.)

(51) " Jab " at thrusting ring (Plate VI).
(52) Direct and oblique " long and short points," and
" jabs," in varying order, at thrusting ring.
(53) When in " jab " position, fend off high and low
" points " made with stick.

3rd Practice. (Pointing at dummy.)

(54) "Jab" from "jab" position.

(55) "Short point" advancing rear foot, and "jab" advancing rear foot.

(56) "Long point" advancing rear foot, "short point" advancing rear foot, and "jab" advancing rear foot (at dummies).

(57) Advance, "long point" and "jab."

(58) Advance, "long point, "short point," and two or more "jabs" (at dummies).

LESSON 5.

1st Practice. (Word of command.)

(59) Class to practise upward butt stroke.

(60) ,, , forward ,, ,,

(61) ,, ,, slash stroke.

(62) ,, ,, overhand butt stroke.

2nd Practice. (Working by eye.)

(63) Upward butt stroke at padded stick (Plate VII).

(64) Forward ,, ,, ,, ,,

(65) Slash stroke at padded stick.

(66) Overhand butt stroke at padded stick (Plate VIII).

(67) Repeat in varying order.

(68) Varied "long points," "short points" and "jabs" at thrusting ring, and left parries, with butt strokes at padded stick,

(69) Trips practised by men working in pairs.

3rd Practice. (On dummy.)

(70) "Point," "jab," &c., at dummies, followed by all butt strokes at light dummies, and introducing kicks and any other form of in-fighting.

SECTION 8.

A Guide for the Trained Soldier's Daily Practice.
(Half-Hour.)

(1) (5 minutes).

    (*a*) "Long points" at hand; Summary (11), (12).
        (Not more than 8 "points" each man.)
    (*b*) "Short points" at hand; Summary 36), (37),
        (38). (Not more than 10 "points" each man.)

(2) (5 minutes.) Steady advance over obstacles and charge 20 yards—about 100 yards in all.

(3) (4 minutes.) Parrying stick and pointing; Summary (23).

(4) (4 minutes.) Butt strokes, each stroke twice; Summary (59), (60), (61), (62); or practise trips, &c.; Summary (69).

(5) (6 minutes.) "Long points," "short points," and "jabs," at thrusting ring, with butt strokes at pad, varied; Summary (68).

(6) (6 minutes.) Final Assault Practice.

N.B.—At least one counter charge practice should be carried out after each individual practice.

PLATE I. "ON GUARD." LESSON 1: SUMMARY (3).

PLATE II. "LONG POINT." LESSON I; SUMMARY (14).

PLATE III. "WITHDRAWAL." LESSON 1; SUMMARY (7), (b).

PLATE IV. "SHORT POINT." LESSON III; SUMMARY (30).

PLATE V. "JAB." LESSON IV ; SUMMARY (45) & (56).

PLATE VI. "JAB" AT THRUSTING RING. LESSON IV; SUMMARY (51).

PLATE VII. UPWARD BUTT STROKE. LESSON V; SUMMARY (63).

PLATE VIII.   OVERHAND BUTT STROKE.   LESSON V;
SUMMARY (66).

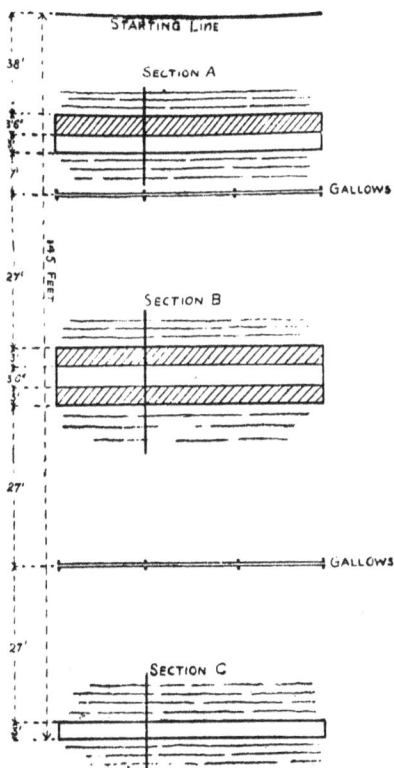

**Diagram 1.—Type of Simple " Final Assault Prac ice "
Course used at the Hd.-Qrs. Gymnasium, Alde shot.**

It is attacked both ways, and the positions of the trench sa k
dummies are varied.

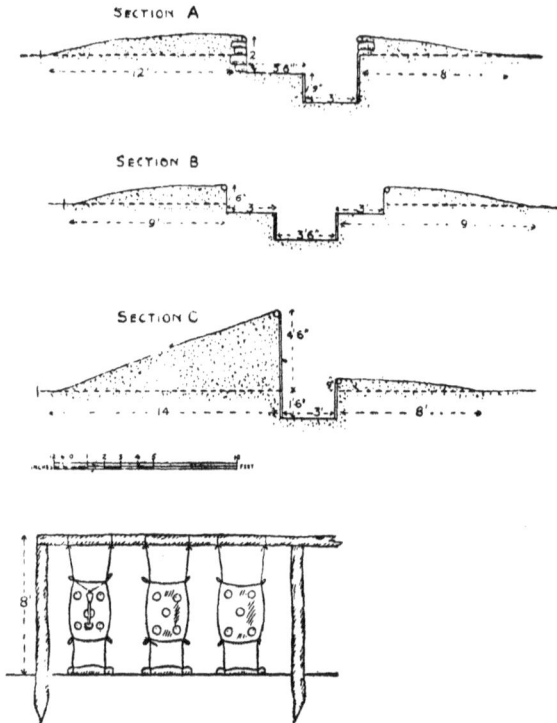

**Diagram I.—Type of Simple " Final Assault Practice"
Course used at the Hd.-Qrs. Gymnasium, Aldershot.**

It is attacked both ways, and the positions of the trench sack
dummies are varied.

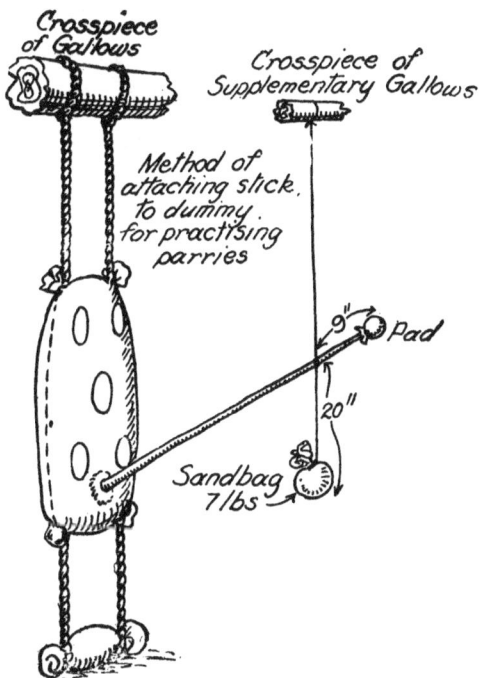

Crosspiece of Gallows

Crosspiece of Supplementary Gallows

Method of attaching stick to dummy for practising parries

9"

Pad

20"

Sandbag 7 lbs

5-inch s akes, 2 feet 3 inches apart should be placed 2 feet in front of the pad. When the attacker passes between them the pad and stick covers the "mark" to be transfixed, thus ensuring that the "opponent's weapon" has to be firmly parried.

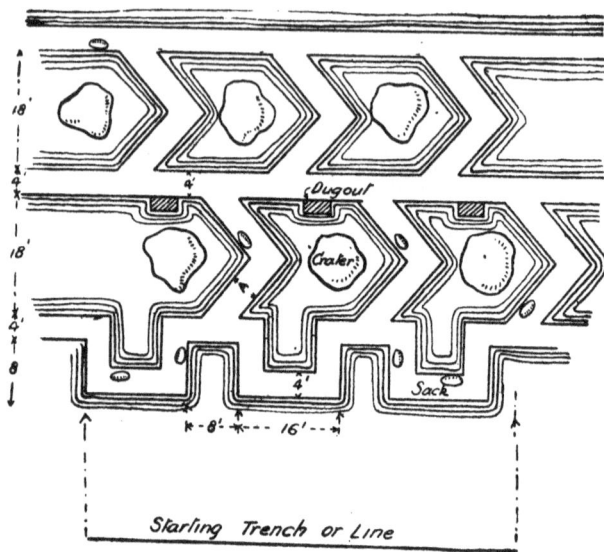

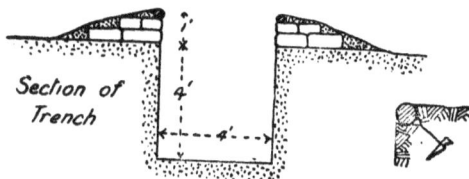

Diagram 2.—Example of Short Communication Trenches.

Which should form part of the usual Final Assault Practice course, where, owing to lack of ground, a "labyrinth" for daily practice with the bayonet in the confined space of a trench cannot be constructed within a convenient distance. On arrival in France drafts are tested in trench bayonet work.

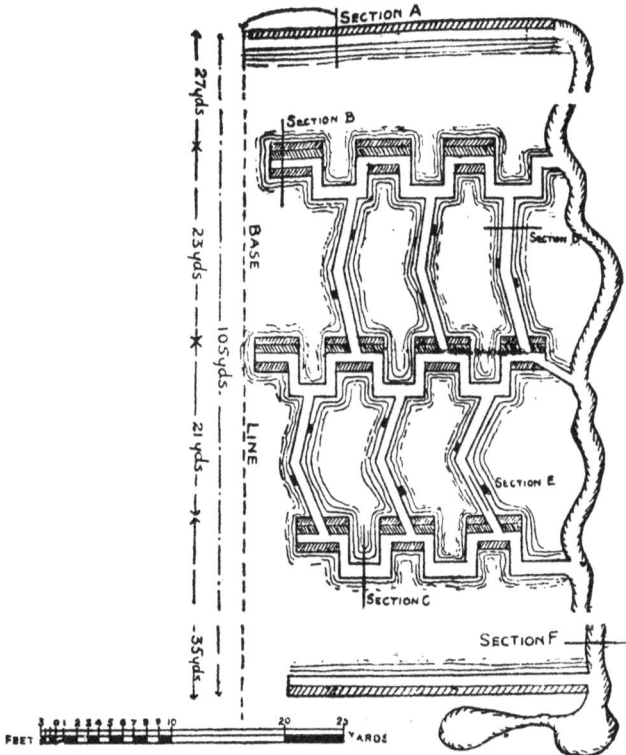

Diagram 3.—Types of "Nursery" Labyrinth used at the Hd.-Qrs. Gymnasium, Aldershot.

The positions of the sack dummies are frequently changed. The ground between the trenches is pitted with "craters" containing dummies, and the men practised in clearing such "crumped" ground as well as in clearing the trenches.

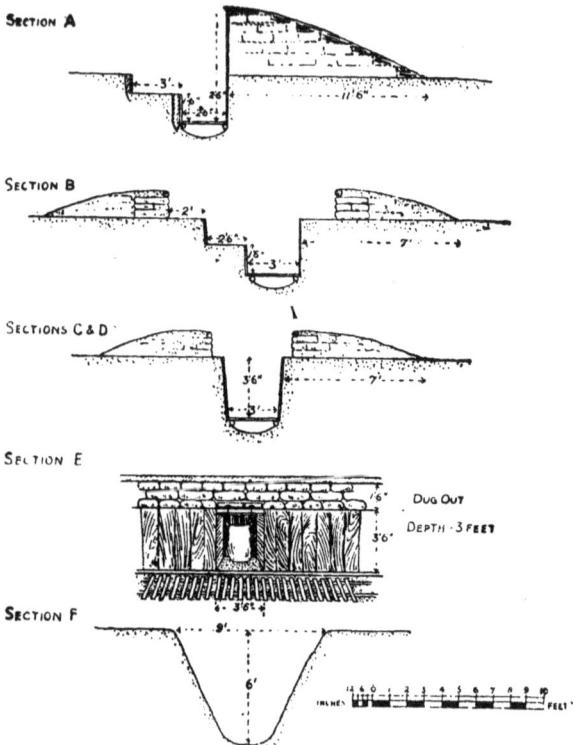

SECTION A

SECTION B

SECTIONS C & D

SECTION E

DUG OUT

DEPTH · 3 FEET

SECTION F

Diagram 3.—Type of " Nursery " Labyrinth used at the Hd.-
Qrs. Gymnasium, Aldershot.

The positions of the sack dummies are frequently changed. The ground
between the trenches is pitted with "craters" containing dummies, and
the men practised in clearing such "crumped" ground as well as in clearing
the trenches.

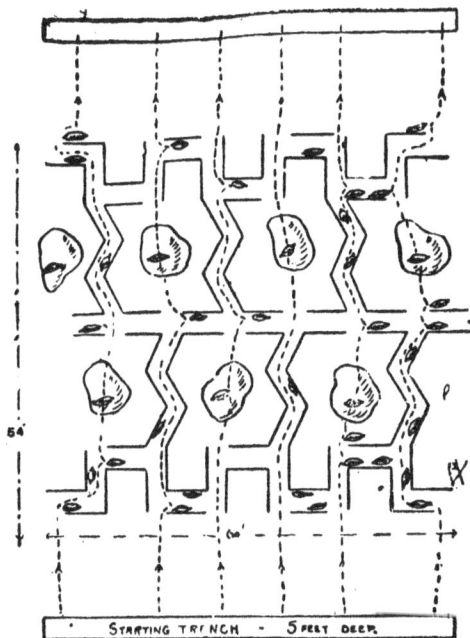

STARTING TRENCH - 5 FEET DEEP.

54'

Diagram 4. — " Overground Labyrinth " for Practice in Wet Weather.

It can be constructed with six-foot hurdles, or canvas screens, or any materials which will give the approximate shape and the narrow limits of trenches. The example above requires 102 six-foot hurdles, which may be set up on fresh ground, and also made to represent various schemes of trenches. The sack dummies should be placed in such a position that the attacker does not see them until he is upon them. Six extra communicating trenches may take the place of craters.

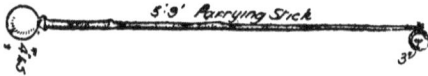

Fig. 5.—Parrying-stick with " Thrusting Ring " and " Pad."

For use :—

(*a*) On the "master and pupil" principle, for practising in two ranks the "Long Point," "Short Point," and "Jab,' according to the position of the ring, alternating with butt strokes and kicks at the pad, according to its position.

(*b*) In charging practice, when both ranks, extended to 3 yards' interval and 20 yards' distance, use the padded ends. Men of one rank charge at a steady double and "point" at opposite men, who "parry." Charging rank halts 20 yards beyond, turns about and charges again, the other rank facing about to meet it. The slight lateral movement required to "parry" is clearly demonstrated in this practice.

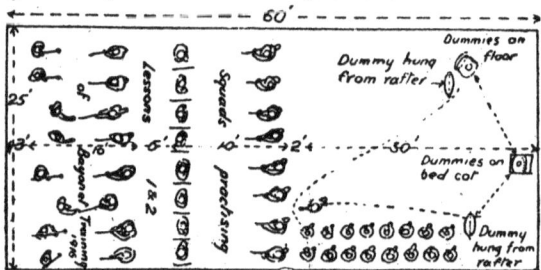

Diagram 6.—Plan of Distribution of Bayonet Training Squads in a Barrack-room in Wet Weather.

Sack dummies can be hung from rafters or frames constructed for the purpose, or be laid *two deep* on bed cots or upon the floor.